F☉CUS ON
Comprehension *1*

Louis Fidge

Nelson

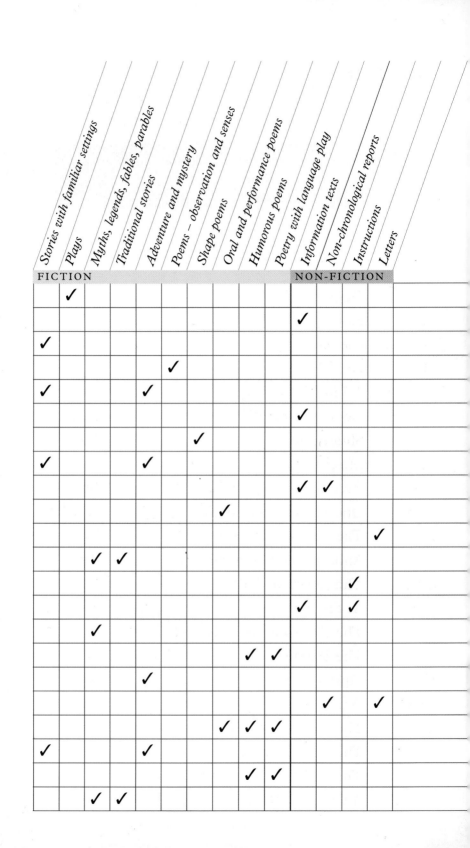

Stories with familiar settings	Plays	Myths, legends, fables, parables	Traditional stories	Adventure and mystery	Poems – observation and senses	Shape poems	Oral and performance poems	Humorous poems	Poetry with language play	Information texts	Non-chronological reports	Instructions	Letters
FICTION										NON-FICTION			
	✓												
										✓			
✓													
				✓									
✓			✓										
										✓			
					✓								
✓			✓										
										✓	✓		
						✓							
												✓	
		✓	✓										
											✓		
										✓		✓	
	✓												
							✓	✓					
			✓										
											✓	✓	
						✓	✓	✓					
✓			✓										
							✓	✓					
		✓	✓										

2

Contents

UNIT 1   Oggy the Caveman

Think ahead

What sort of things did cave dwellers do?
What were their lives like?

NARRATOR: *Long ago, in a damp cave, there lived a group of cave dwellers. Their life was hard and tough, and so were most of them, except one, called Oggy. He was different. He didn't like living in a cave.*

OGGY: I'm fed up with living here. Why can't we find a better place to live?

UGGY: But we have always lived in a cave.

OGGY: I hate all the creepy crawlies and the bats that fly everywhere. The cave is damp and draughty and my bones hurt from sleeping on rocks.

UGGY: You are going soft! There's nothing wrong with our cave.

OGGY: Well I'm going to brighten it up a bit, and paint some pictures on the walls.

NARRATOR: *The others laughed at Oggy and made fun of him. Some of them picked up their clubs and went off to hunt for their dinner.*

OGGY: I hate hunting. I'm going to plant some seeds and grow my own food.

UGGY: *(With a sigh)* Why can't you be a *real* caveman, like the rest of us?

➡ *Thinking back*

Choose the correct answer.
1 Oggy lived in a   a) house   b) cave   c) tent
2 Oggy slept on a   a) rock   b) pillow   c) sack
3 When they went hunting the cavemen carried
   a) bags   b) sticks   c) clubs
4 Oggy liked to plant
   a) seeds   b) flowers   c) plants

➡ *Thinking about it*

Write the answers to these questions in your book.
1 Name three things Oggy did not like about living in a cave.
2 Oggy liked to do some things that the other cavemen didn't. Name them.
3 Why do you think cavemen went hunting with clubs?
4 Write the opposites of these adjectives:
   a) hard   b) cold   c) nice   d) kind   e) tough

➡ *Thinking it through*

1 How can you tell this is a play?
2 Explain what a narrator is.
3 If you were playing Oggy in the play, how would you know when it was your turn to speak?
4 Write a few more lines of the play. Set it out properly.

UNIT 2   Hot Air Balloons

Think ahead

What would it be like to float up high in the sky in a hot air balloon?

The hot air balloon goes wherever the wind blows it.

The balloon is made of nylon.

Hot air is lighter than cold air. When a balloon is filled with hot air it floats.

The pilot burns gas from a large metal bottle. The hotter the air is inside the balloon, the higher it rises.

The wicker basket is made of branches from a willow tree.

Thinking back

Say whether each sentence is true (T) or false (F).
1 The balloon is made of cloth.
2 Hot air is lighter than cold air.
3 Gas is kept in a large metal bottle.
4 The basket is made of plastic.
5 The hot air balloon goes wherever the wind blows it.

Thinking about it

Answer these questions in your book.
1 What is the basket for?
2 What is the large metal bottle of gas for?
3 Why is the balloon filled with hot air?
4 Why do you think the pilot of the balloon checks the wind direction before setting off?

Thinking it through

Answer these questions in your book.
1 The pilot of the balloon keeps in touch with someone in a car by radio. The car follows the balloon. Why do you think this is?
2 Explain what you think some of the dangers of hot air ballooning might be.
3 Explain why you think some people love hot air ballooning.

UNIT 3 Cleaning Up

Think ahead

Are you a tidy person? Who keeps things tidy in your house? Does anyone ever moan if your room gets untidy?

Perfect peace ... rudely shattered!

From *Another Helping of Chips* by Shirley Hughes

8

➤ *Thinking back*

Answer these questions in your book.
1 What is the name of the boy?
2 Is he a tidy or an untidy boy?
3 Who is cleaning up the house?
4 What sort of pet does Chips have?
5 Does Chips have any younger brothers or sisters?
6 What does Chips call his grandfather?

➤ *Thinking about it*

Answer these questions in your book.
1 How can you tell the vacuum cleaner is noisy?
2 Why doesn't the cat like dust?
3 Why is the cat going into the garden?
4 Why do you think Chips' mum calls his space station 'rubbish'?
5 What do you think is in the sack that Chips' mum is carrying out of his bedroom?

➤ *Thinking it through*

Answer these questions in your book.
1 Describe the sort of mood Chips' mum is in.
2 How can you tell Chips does not like tidying up?
3 What do you think Grandpa means when he says, 'We just have to grit our teeth till it's over'?
4 How can you tell what the cat might be thinking?

UNIT 4 Gone

Think ahead

How would you feel if your best friend had to move?

In a big house across the way
Lived my friend Jane, until today,
Six men this morning, in a van,
Came after breakfast, and began
To pack up all the beds and chairs,
The nice red carpet on the stairs,
And all the things I used to see,
When Jane invited me for tea.

They took the dishes and the plates,
And packed them all into wooden crates.
They took Jane's toboggan, dolls and all.
They took the big clock from the hall.
They took the carpet, tied with strings,
And pots and pans and kitchen things.
They took the sofa where we played
(And where I slept, the night I stayed.)

Cupboards, chests and kitchen stools,
Cooker, fridge and gardening tools,
Jane's red bike – I don't know how
They got them in that van. But now
They've gone, and shut the big front door,
And I can't call there anymore.
It's sad to think, that from today,
I'll never go to Jane's to play.

From *The Tinder Box Assembly Book*

Thinking back

Choose the best ending for each sentence.
1 Jane lived   a) across the way   b) next door
   c) in the next street
2 The removal men came   a) at lunch time
   b) before breakfast   c) after breakfast
3 The men took the big clock from
   a) the front room   b) the hall   c) the kitchen
4 Jane's bike was   a) red   b) blue   c) green

Thinking about it

1 Make a list of ten things the removal men put
   in the van.
2 How do you know the writer often went into
   Jane's house?
3 Did the writer ever stay at Jane's house?
   How do you know?
4 What was the last thing the removal men did?

Thinking it through

Answer these questions in your book.
1 How can you tell the writer felt sad Jane was
   moving?
2 Do you think the writer was a boy or a girl?
   Why?
3 How did the poem make you feel? Why?
4 What sort of things do you think Jane will miss?

UNIT 5　A Lion at School

Think ahead

What would you think if a lion came to your school?

A little girl made friends with a lion and took him to school with her.

All the big boys were running about, and the very biggest boy, Jack Tall, came running towards the little girl.

'Go away,' said the lion. 'You might knock my friend over. Go away.'

'Shan't,' said Jack Tall.

The little girl got behind the lion. The lion began to swish his tail: Swish! Swish! Jack Tall was running closer and closer and closer. The lion growled. Then Jack Tall saw the lion's teeth as sharp as skewers and knives. He stopped running. He stood still. He stared.

The lion opened his mouth wider – so wide that Jack Tall could see his throat, deep and dark like a tunnel to go into. Jack Tall went pale.

Then the lion roared.

He roared and ROARED and he **ROARED**.

Jack Tall turned round and ran and ran and ran – out through the playground – out through the school gates – along the streets. He never stopped running until he got home to his mother.

From *Lion at School* by Philippa Pearce

> *Thinking back*

Say whether each sentence is true (T) or false (F).

1 Jack Tall was a big boy.
2 The lion asked Jack Tall to come and play.
3 When the lion growled, Jack Tall could see the lion's teeth.
4 Jack Tall ran back into school.

> *Thinking about it*

These sentences tell the story but they are in the wrong order. Write them out in the correct order.

- The lion started to swish his tail.
- Jack Tall ran home to his mother.
- Jack Tall came up to the little girl.
- The lion roared very loudly.
- The lion told Jack to go away.

> *Thinking it through*

Answer these questions in your book.

1 Small children can sometimes find the playground a frightening place. Why do you think this is?
2 What sort of boy do you think Jack Tall was?
3 Do you think the way the lion treated Jack served him right? Explain your answer.

UNIT 6   Good Manners

Think ahead

What sort of things do you think are polite?
What sort of things are bad-mannered?

Introduction

Customs vary from country to country. It is important to choose the correct greeting or you may upset someone. For example, in some places in Africa people greet each other by spitting in the face. This would not be polite in our country!

Kissing

In the Middle Ages kissing was a common greeting. When a Dutchman visited an English family in the sixteenth century he was expected to kiss every member of the family, including the cat!

Shaking hands

Do you know why people shake hands with their right hands? In olden times soldiers usually held their weapons in their right hands. To offer an empty right hand was a sign that the soldier came in peace.

Bowing is a mark of respect in most places. In Japan people keep bowing to each other until one of them stands up straight again. Then the other can stop.

Thinking back

Copy and complete each sentence.

1 In some places in _____ people greet each other by spitting in the face.
2 In the Middle Ages _____ was a common greeting.
3 In olden times soldiers used to hold their weapons in their _____ hands.
4 In _____ people bow to each other when they meet.

Thinking about it

Now answer these questions.

1 Why is it important to learn how to greet someone correctly?
2 Why was the Dutchman surprised in the sixteenth century?
3 Why do you think the Japanese greet each other in the way they do?

Thinking it through

Make up sensible answers to these questions.

1 Which part did you find most interesting? Give a reason.
2 Which two things quickly helped you to find the information on the opposite page?
3 What would make a good heading for the last paragraph?
4 List some other things that show *bad* manners.

UNIT 7   Shape Poems

Think ahead

Look at the pictures. What do you think each poem is going to be about?

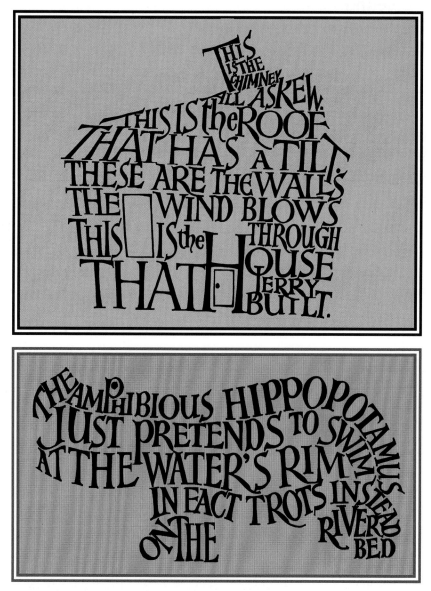

From *The Scholastic Collections* by Jenny Morris

> ## Thinking back

Copy and complete each sentence.
1 The first poem is about a _____ .
2 The roof of the house has a _____ .
3 The wind blows through the _____ .
4 The second poem is about a _____ .
5 The hippopotamus just pretends to _____ .

> ## Thinking about it

1 Write what you think 'The chimney is all askew' means.
2 Why do you think the wind blows through the walls?
3 Was the builder of the house any good? Give your reasons.
4 Guess what you think 'amphibious' means.
5 When a hippopotamus is in the river, how much of it do you see?

> ## Thinking it through

1 Explain what is special about the presentation of the poems.
2 Write one of the poems out in lines as poems are normally set out. Which way of setting out the poems do you prefer? Why?
3 Which of the two shape poems do you like best?
4 Try to make a shape poem of your own about a snake or a tall factory chimney.

UNIT 8   Magic!

Think ahead

What do you think this story is going to be about?

Lottie had a plaster on her knee. She was worried it would hurt when it was taken off. Her Mum said she would do it by magic!

Lottie's mother sat down beside her. 'Close your eyes,' she said. Lottie closed them. 'Now what can you see?'

'Dark.'

'Look harder. Can you see any stars in the darkness?'

'Oh yes!' said Lottie. 'Stars and moonlight. And everything is covered with thick snow.'

'Is it frosty?'

'Yes. And it's very cold.' Lottie snuggled closer to her mother. But she kept her eyes tight shut.

'Can you see anything else?' her mother asked, as she put her arm round Lottie.

'A castle. A fairy castle made out of crystal glass. It's beautiful!' Lottie gazed and gazed at the picture behind her closed eyelids, until her mother said, 'Now, why don't you look at your knee?' So Lottie did.

'My plaster has gone! My plaster has gone! How did you do it?' 'By magic,' said her mother.

From *Mother's Magic* by Susan Hill

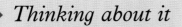

Thinking back

Complete these sentences in a sensible way.

1 Lottie had a plaster on her _____ .

2 Lottie's mum said she would take the plaster off by _____ .

3 Lottie sat down _____ her mum on the bed.

4 When Lottie opened her eyes the plaster had _____ .

Thinking about it

Answer these questions in your book.

1 Did Lottie *really* want her plaster off?

2 List three things Lottie could see when she closed her eyes.

3 Why did Lottie snuggle closer to her mum?

4 Why was Lucy surprised when she looked at her knee when she opened her eyes?

Thinking it through

Answer these questions in your book.

1 Explain how you think Lottie's mum managed to get her plaster off without Lottie knowing.

2 Lottie's mum said it was done by magic. Do you agree?

3 Would you say Lottie had a good imagination?

4 How would *you* answer the question, 'What is magic?'

UNIT 9 Recommending Books

Think ahead

How do you choose books to read? By their covers, by the 'blurb' written at the back? Do you ever choose books that someone has recommended to you? Why?

An author recommended two very different animal books to his readers. This is what he said about them:

The Hodgeheg,
Dick King-Smith - *Antelope*
Max thinks he's a hodgeheg! He's a little mixed up since he got knocked over, or, as he says in the book, 'Something bot me on the hittom and then I headed my bang.' The problem is that Max is a hedgehog, but his ambition is to cross the road safely. The book is full of his hilarious adventures trying to do so. Does he manage? Read it and see!

Focus on Mammals,
Jane Parker - *Gloucester Press*

This slim, easy-to-read, hard-backed book is full of short, snappy facts about animals. You can find out:
• why zebras have stripes (page 12)!
• which animals can run fastest (page 12)!
• why wolves have such a bad name (page 22)!
This book is brilliant. It has stunning photos and drawings that will leap off the page at you!

Thinking back

Match up the sentence beginnings and endings.

1 *The Hodgeheg* is by   Max the hedgehog.
2 *The Hodgeheg* is about   Dick King-Smith.
3 *Focus on Mammals* is   in *Focus on Mammals*.
4 You can discover why   an information book.
  zebras are striped

Thinking about it

1 What have the two books in common?
2 What is the name of the publisher of each book?
3 Why do you think Max is a little mixed up?
4 The pictures in *Focus on Mammals* 'leap off the
  page at you!' What does that mean?

Thinking it through

1 Which book do you like the sound of best? Why?
2 Why and how does the reviewer use exclamation
  marks?
3 How does the review try to persuade you to read
  The Hodgeheg?
4 The review of *Focus on Mammals* uses a mixture
  of fact and opinion. Write a paragraph about the
  book but only use some of the facts given.

UNIT 10 One Smiling Grandma

Think ahead

Look at the title. Do you think this is going to be a happy poem? Why?

One smiling Grandma in a rocking chair,
Two yellow bows tied on braided hair.
Three humming birds sipping nectar sweet.
Four steel drums tapping out their beat.
Five flying fish gliding through the air.
Six market ladies selling their wares.
Seven conch shells I find on the beach.
Eight sugar apples, just out of reach.
Nine hairy coconuts, hard and round.
Ten sleepy mongoose
Hush! Not a sound!

From *One Smiling Grandma* by Anne Marie Linden and Lynne Russell

Thinking back

Copy and complete each sentence.
1 There were three _____ .
2 There were eight _____ .
3 There were five _____ .
4 There was one _____ .
5 There were two _____ .

Thinking about it

Answer these questions in your book.
1 What were the coconuts like?
2 What were the drums made of?
3 Where were the six ladies?
4 What sort of shells were on the beach?
5 What would happen if there was too much noise?

Thinking it through

Answer these questions in your book.
1 What words tell you that the drums were being played?
2 What do you think 'sipping nectar sweet' means?
3 The poem was written in the Caribbean. How can you tell?
4 Write something you liked or disliked about the poem.

UNIT 11 The Royal Invitation

Think ahead

What is an invitation? Do you like being invited to things?
What do you know about Cinderella?

His Highness Prince Charming
is pleased to invite Cinderella
to a Grand Ball at the Royal Palace.

It will take place on
Saturday October 25th at 10pm.

Please wear a ball gown and
glass slippers.

The Prince's Golden Coach will
be sent to collect you.

The Prince eagerly awaits your reply.

Signed
Your most humble admirer,

Prince Charming

➡ *Thinking back*

Answer these questions in your book.
1 Who sent the invitation?
2 Who was the invitation for?
3 What was it an invitation to?
4 Where is the Grand Ball to take place?
5 When will it take place?
6 How will Cinderella be collected?

➡ *Thinking about it*

Answer these questions in your book.
1 Will the ball take place in the morning, afternoon or at night? How do you know?
2 Do you think people could go to the Ball in ordinary clothes? Explain your answer.
3 Why do you think the Prince is sending his own coach to collect Cinderella?

➡ *Thinking it through*

Answer these questions in your book.
1 In what ways is this invitation different from the ones you get?
2 How can you tell the Prince is keen to see Cinderella?
3 If you admire someone do you *like* them a little, quite a lot or a great deal?
4 Would you be pleased to receive such an invitation? Why?

UNIT 12 Anancy and Common Sense

Think ahead

Who do you think Anancy is?
Can you guess what the story might be about?

Anancy thought that if he collected all the common sense in the world he would become the most powerful.

He collected and collected, and all that he found he put in a large calabash (pot). Then he began to worry that someone might steal it so he decided to hide it at the top of a tree.

He tied a rope around the pot and tied the rope around his neck and rested the pot on his stomach. When he tried to climb the tree he found that the calabash kept getting in his way.

Suddenly he heard a little boy laughing behind him. 'How silly you are, Anancy,' he laughed. Why don't you have the calabash behind you when you climb?'

Anancy was so annoyed to hear this bit of common sense coming from a little boy that he threw the calabash to the ground. It broke into pieces and the common sense it contained was scattered all over the world.

Nearly everyone got a bit of it. Did you?

Caribbean traditional tale

Copy these sentences. Think of a suitable word to go in each gap.

Anancy wanted to collect all the common sense in the __1__ so he could become the most __2__ . He put the common sense in a __3__ and stuffed dry leaves over it. He tried to carry the calabash up to the __4__ of a tree to __5__ it. Anancy __6__ the pot and __7__ it.

➡️ *Thinking about it*

Write sentences to answer these questions in your book.

1 Why did Anancy want to hide the calabash at the top of the tree?
2 Why did Anancy have difficulty climbing the tree?
3 Why did Anancy get annoyed?
4 What happened when he got annoyed?

➡️ *Thinking it through*

1 Which of the adjectives below could be used to describe Anancy?
   powerful   greedy   foolish   silly   wise   careful
2 What do you think of Anancy?
3 Do you think it is possible for anyone to have all the common sense in the world? Explain your answer.

UNIT 13 The Country Code

Think ahead

What rules do you have in your school?
The Country Code is a set of rules for the countryside.

- Enjoy the countryside but take care of it.
- Shut all gates behind you.
- Keep your dog under control.
- Take your litter home.
- Do not make a lot of noise.
- Prevent fires.
- Keep all water clean.
- Protect all wildlife, plants and trees.
- Leave animals, crops and farm machinery alone.
- Keep to the footpaths.

➤ *Thinking back*

Answer these questions in your book.
What should you:
1 shut?
2 keep under control?
3 take home?
4 protect?
5 leave alone?

➤ *Thinking about it*

Answer these questions in your book.
Why do you think it is important that you:
1 shut all gates?
2 keep your dog under control?
3 do not make a lot of noise?
4 keep to the footpath?
5 prevent fires?

➤ *Thinking it through*

Answer these questions in your book.
1 Choose which you think are the three most important rules. Write them in order of importance.
2 Why do you think it is important to have a country code?
3 What do you think the word 'code' means?

UNIT 14 At the Fair

Think ahead

*What sort of things would you expect to find at
a Fun Fair?*

*In the summer Abdi and Shireen were on holiday at the
seaside with their Mum and Dad. The best day they had
was when they went to the fun fair.*

The Twister

Ghost Train

Big
Wheel

Hot
Dogs

Bouncy
Castle

Log Flume

The Wall
of Death

Dodgem
Cars

Café   Toilets

Ice
Creams

➡ *Thinking back*

Copy and complete these sentences with suitable words.

1 ____ and ____ were on holiday.
2 They went on holiday in the ____ with their ____ .
3 The family had a holiday at the ____ .
4 At the seaside there was a ____ ____ .

➡ *Thinking about it*

1 When you come in the entrance
   a) what two rides are on either side of you?
   b) are straight ahead of you?
2 Is the Log Flume at the centre or to the right of the fair?
3 What is between the Dodgem Cars and the Ghost Train?
4 Where are the toilets?
5 What can you buy to eat at the fair?

➡ *Thinking it through*

1 Are there any other things missing that you would like to see at a fun fair?
2 Imagine you have only enough money for four rides. What would you choose to go on?
3 How easy do you think it is to find your way round the fair in the plan? Why?
4 What do you like about fun fairs?

UNIT 15 The Dog and His Reflection

Think ahead

Who do you think the main character is going to be in this story?

A dog was feeling very proud of himself. He had found a large piece of meat and was carrying it away in his mouth, so he could eat it in peace somewhere.

He came to a stream and began to cross over a narrow plank which led from one bank to the other. Suddenly he stopped and looked down. In the water he saw his own reflection shining up at him.

The dog did not realise he was looking at himself. He thought he was looking at another dog with a large piece of meat in its mouth.

'Hello, that piece of meat is bigger than mine,' he thought. 'I'll grab it and run.'

At that he dropped his own piece of meat in order to snatch the piece the other dog had. Of course his piece of meat fell into the stream and sank to the bottom, leaving the dog with nothing.

Aesop's Fable

➡ *Thinking back*

Choose the best words to complete the sentences.
1 In his mouth the dog was carrying (a bone/
   a piece of meat).
2 The dog came to a (stream/river).
3 The dog walked across a (log/plank).
4 In the water the dog saw his (reflection/shadow).
5 The dog dropped the (meat/stick) in the water.

➡ *Thinking about it*

Answer these questions in your book.
1 Why was the dog proud of himself?
2 Why was he carrying the meat away?
3 What made him stop?
4 What did he think when he saw his reflection?
5 Why did the dog let go of his own piece of meat?

➡ *Thinking it through*

Answer these questions in your book.
1 The dog felt proud of himself. What sort of
   things make you feel proud?
2 Do you think the dog was greedy or silly? Why?
3 This story is a fable. That means it tries to teach
   us a lesson. Which of these do you think this story
   tries to teach us?
   a) Do not try to be too clever.
   b) Be happy with what you have got.
   c) Look before you leap.

UNIT 16 The Surprise

Think ahead

Do you like surprises?
What is the nicest surprise you have ever had?
What do you think the surprise could be in this poem?

I met a lion in the park,
I took him home for tea,
But when I'd fed him bread and jam
He wouldn't play with me.

I met a camel in the rain,
We both got very wet,
But when I took him home to Mum,
He wouldn't be my pet.

I met a monkey in the street,
She had a baby, too,
But when I asked them home for lunch,
They went to Timbuctoo.

I met my Daddy in the shop,
He'd bought me a surprise.
It had a little curly tail,
And big brown puppy eyes.

From *First Rhymes* by Lucy Coats

Thinking back

Answer these questions in your book.
1 Where was the lion?
2 Where was the camel?
3 Where was the monkey?
4 Where was the father?
5 What was the surprise?

Thinking about it

Answer these questions in your book.
1 What did the lion have for tea?
2 Why did the camel get wet?
3 Was it a mother or father monkey?
  How can you tell?
4 What time of day was it when the monkeys
  went to Timbuctoo?
5 What colour were the puppy's eyes?
6 What sort of a tail did it have?

Thinking it through

Answer these questions in your book.
1 Read these two statements. Say which you agree
  with and why.
  a) There really was a lion, a camel and a monkey.
  b) The child is making it up.
2 What sort of shop was the father in?
  How do you know?
3 Did you like the end of the poem? Say why.

UNIT 17 Flying

Think ahead

Have you ever heard the story of Peter Pan?
Do you know what happens in the story?

By this time Peter had blown magic dust all over the children, and was showing them how to fly.

'Just wriggle your shoulders and let go!' he cried, swooping round the room. One by one they took off from their beds and followed him, a bit wobbly at first.

Michael shouted 'I flewed! I flewed!'

John called 'Look at me!' bumping the ceiling. He was wearing his Sunday top hat, and looked very funny.

'Oh lovely!' cried Wendy, in mid air near the bathroom.

Mr and Mrs Darling and Nana came along the street and saw the nursery window lighted up. Against the curtains, they could see the shadows of three little figures in night clothes, circling round and round, not on the floor, but in the air! Not three, but *four*!

They rushed upstairs and burst into the room, just too late. Peter had said 'Follow me!' and soared out into the night, followed by John and Michael and Wendy.

From *Peter Pan* by J M Barrie

➡ *Thinking back*

Choose the best ending for each sentence.
Write the sentences in your book.
1 Peter had some magic (dust, spells)
2 Peter showed the children how to (wobble, fly)
3 John was wearing his (top hat, Sunday clothes)
4 Wendy was flying near the (stairs, bathroom)
5 Mr and Mrs Darling arrived just (in time,
   too late)

➡ *Thinking about it*

These sentences tell the story but are in the
wrong order. Write them in the correct order.
• The children took off from their beds.
• Mr and Mrs Darling rushed up the stairs.
• Peter blew magic dust over the children.
• The children flew out of the nursery window.

➡ *Thinking it through*

1 Do you think Nana was the name of their
   grandmother or their dog?
2 Which child was the youngest? How can you tell?
3 How do you think the children felt when they
   began to fly?
4 How did Mr and Mrs Darling know something
   strange was happening?
5 What do you think Mr and Mrs Darling did
   next?

UNIT 18 Pen Friends

Think ahead

What do you think a pen friend might be?

This is the first letter I have written to my new pen friend. She lives in a different town.

14 Downs Road
Luton
LU2 8RX
18th September 1998

Dear Amy
    I am glad you want to be my penfriend.
I am nearly 8 years old and have black hair.
My Mum sometimes calls me 'Sweety' because
Shirleen means sweet. I like skating and watching
soaps on TV. I love horses. I wish I could have one
of my own. I enjoy listening to music and drawing.
I have a younger brother called Ali but he is a bit
of a pest! My house has a nice garden with lots of
flowers. I hope you will write back soon and tell me
all about yourself.

Love from
        Shirleen

Thinking back

Answer each question with a sentence.
1 Who wrote the letter?
2 Who was the letter to?
3 Where does Shirleen live?
4 Where does Amy live?
5 How many letters has Shirleen written to Amy?

Thinking about it

There are a lot of facts about Shirleen in her letter.
Write a 'fact file' about her. Include at least eight
different facts. Do it like this:

Fact File about Shirleen
Shirleen is eight years old. She has black hair.

Thinking it through

1 Explain what you think a penfriend is.
2 Think of some other things you think Shirleen
   could have told Amy about.
3 Imagine Shirleen had written to you and not to
   Amy. Write a short reply to her, telling her some
   interesting things about yourself.

UNIT 19 The Land of the Bumbley Boo

Think ahead

Do you think there is such a place as the Land of the Bumbley Boo? What sort of place do you think it might be?

In the Land of the Bumbley Boo
The people are red, white and blue,
They never blow noses,
Or ever wear closes,
What a sensible thing to do!

In the Land of the Bumbley Boo
You can buy lemon pie at the zoo;
They give away foxes
In little pink boxes
And bottles of dandelion stew.

In the Land of the Bumbley Boo
You never see a gnu,
But thousands of cats
Wearing trousers and hats
Made of pumpkin and pelican glue!

Chorus
Oh, the Bumbley Boo! the Bumbley Boo!
That's the place for me and you!
So hurry! Let's run!
The train leaves at one!
For the Land of the Bumbley Boo!
The wonderful Bumbley Boo-Boo-Boo!
The wonderful Bumbley BOO!

From *Silly Verse for Kids* by Spike Milligan

➤ *Thinking back*

Copy these sentences and choose a sensible word to fill in each gap.
In the Land of the Bumbley Boo, the people are red, __1__ and blue. At the __2__ you can buy lemon pie. The people give away __3__ in little __4__ boxes. You will see __5__ of cats there. The cats wear trousers and __6__ .

➤ *Thinking about it*

Answer these questions in your book.
1 There are three things the people never do. What are they?
2 What might you find in a bottle?
3 What do you think a gnu is?
4 What are the cats' trousers and hats made of?
5 How can you get to Bumbley Boo?

➤ *Thinking it through*

Answer these questions in your book.
1 Did you like the poem? Why?
2 The poem is a 'nonsense' poem. What do you think this means?
3 Write the word in the poem that rhymes with:
   a) noses   b) foxes   c) cats   d) run
   e) Write the words that rhyme with Boo.
4 What other things do you think you might see in the Land of the Bumbley Boo?

UNIT 20 The Whales' Song

Think ahead

Do you think whales really can sing?

Lilly's Grandmother was always telling Lilly stories about the wonderful whales that lived a long time ago. In her dreams, Lilly heard the whales singing to her and calling her name.

Next morning Lilly went down to the ocean. She went where no-one fished or swam or sailed their boats. She walked to the end of the old jetty, the water was empty and still. Out of her pocket she took a yellow flower and dropped it in the water. 'This is for you,' she called into the air.

That night, Lilly awoke suddenly.

The room was bright with moonlight. She sat up and listened. The house was quiet. Lilly climbed out of bed and went to the window. She could hear something in the distance, on the far side of the hill.

She raced outside and down to the shore. Her heart was pounding as she reached the sea.

There, enormous in the ocean, were the whales.

They leapt and jumped and spun across the moon.

Their singing filled up the night.

Lilly saw her yellow flower dancing on the spray.

From *The Whales' Song* by Dyan Sheldon

➤ Thinking back

Answer these questions in your book.
1 Who told Lilly stories about whales?
2 What did the whales do in Lilly's dreams?
3 What did Lilly drop on the water?
4 Where did Lilly go when she woke up?
5 What did Lilly see in the ocean?

➤ Thinking about it

Answer these questions in your book.
1 Why do you think Lilly dreamt about whales?
2 Why did Lilly drop a flower on the water?
3 What do you think made Lilly wake up?
4 How can you tell that Lilly ran quickly to the sea shore?

➤ Thinking it through

1 What do these words mean:
   a) jetty   b) ocean   c) spray?
2 How do you think Lilly felt when she saw the whales? Why?
3 Explain what you think these phrases from the story mean:
   a) enormous in the ocean
   b) spun across the moon?
4 What is the loveliest dream you ever had?

UNIT 21 The Owl and the Pussy-Cat

Think ahead
How can you tell this is a poem? Who wrote it?

The Owl and the Pussy-Cat went to sea
In a beautiful pea-green boat,
They took some honey, and plenty of money,
Wrapped up in a five-pound note.
The Owl looked up to the stars above,
And sang to a small guitar,
'O lovely Pussy! O Pussy my love,
What a beautiful Pussy you are
You are,
You are!
What a beautiful Pussy you are!'

Pussy said to the Owl, 'You elegant fowl!
How charmingly sweet you sing!
Oh let us get married! Too long we have tarried!
But what shall we do for a ring?'
They sailed away for a year and a day,
To the land where the Bong-tree grows,
And there in a wood a Piggy-wig stood
With a ring at the end of his nose,
His nose,
His nose,
With a ring at the end of his nose.

From *The Owl and the Pussy-Cat* by Edward Lear

▶ *Thinking back*

Say if these sentences are true or false.
1 The Owl and Pussy-Cat had a blue boat.
2 They took lots of money on their trip.
3 The Pussy-Cat played a guitar.
4 The Pussy-Cat said they should get married.
5 They sailed in their boat for over a year.

▶ *Thinking about it*

Answer these questions in your book.
1 How can you tell the Owl is in love?
2 How can you tell the Pussy-Cat liked the Owl?
3 What sort of trees were in the wood?
4 Where did Piggy-wig have his ring?

▶ *Thinking it through*

Answer these questions in your book.
1 Did the Owl really sing 'to a small guitar'?
  What does this mean?
2 Was there anything you found hard to
  understand in the poem? What?
3 The last verse has been left out. Try to find it in
  a poetry book.
4 How many verses is the whole poem divided into?
5 Name the four characters mentioned in the
  poem. Who are they?

UNIT 22 A Creation Story

Think ahead
What do you think creation stories are?

A Yoruba Creation Story
(The Yoruba tribe live in Nigeria, in Africa.)
In the beginning there was no dry land, only water and marshes. Olorun lived in the sky with the other gods. At night they used to swing down on spiders' webs and play in the marshes.

One day Olorun decided to make some dry land. He gave Orisha Nla a snail shell full of earth and a five-toed hen and told him to go and make a firm dry place to walk. On his way, Orisha Nla met some gods having a party so he stopped to join in the fun. His younger brother, Oduduwa, took the earth and the hen, and came down from the sky. He threw down the earth and the hen began to scratch around in it until it had made some dry land. Then Oduduwa planted all kinds of seeds and trees, which would be good for animals and humans.

At this point Orisha Nla woke up and saw that the earth had been created. He came down to see who had done it. Oduduwa and Orisha Nla argued and fought over who the earth belonged to. Olorun had to intervene and pull them apart. He decided that Oduduwa should be king of the earth and Orisha Nla should mould human bodies. Olorun sent the Thunder God to keep the peace between them.

➤ Thinking back

Choose the correct ending for each sentence.
According to the Yoruba creation story:

1 Olorun and the gods used to swing down to earth on:
   a) spiders' webs   b) ropes   c) vines
2 Orisha Nla did not:
   a) go to a party   b) go to sleep
   c) do as he was told.
3 It was Oduduwa who made the:
   a) sky   b) dry land   c) rain

➤ Thinking about it

1 Why do you think Olorun decided to make some dry land one day?
2 Why do you think Oduduwa took over the job that Orisha Nla had been given to do?
3 Why did Olorun have to send the Thunder God to 'keep the peace'?

➤ Thinking it through

1 What did you think of the story? Why?
2 Why do you think different people explain the creation of the world in different ways?
3 Do you think these events ever really happened? Give your reasons.
4 Some people call these types of stories 'creation myths'. What do you think this means?